Log on to www.av2books.com

AV² by Weigl brings you media enhanced books that support active learning. Go to www.av2books.com, and enter the special code found on page 2 of this book. You will gain access to enriched and enhanced content that supplements and complements this book. Content includes video, audio, weblinks, quizzes, a slide show, and activities.

AV² Online Navigation

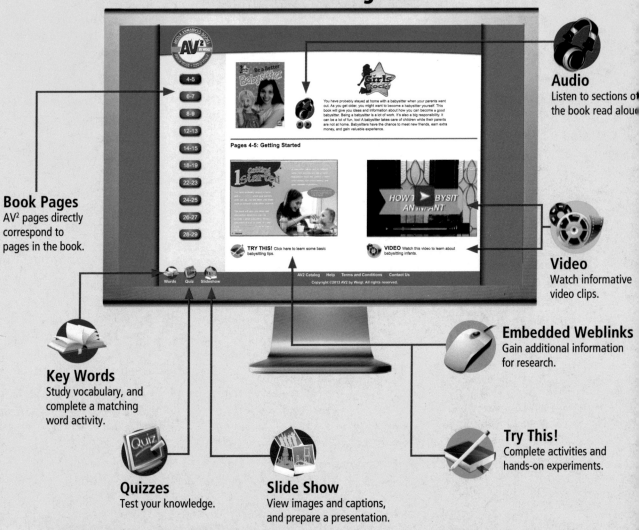

Book Pages
AV² pages directly correspond to pages in the book.

Key Words
Study vocabulary, and complete a matching word activity.

Quizzes
Test your knowledge.

Slide Show
View images and captions, and prepare a presentation.

Audio
Listen to sections of the book read aloud.

Video
Watch informative video clips.

Embedded Weblinks
Gain additional information for research.

Try This!
Complete activities and hands-on experiments.

AV² was built to bridge the gap between print and digital. We encourage you to tell us what you like and what you want to see in the future.

Sign up to be an AV² Ambassador at www.av2books.com/ambassador.

Key Words

babysitter a person who takes care of children while their parents are out

communication a spoken or written message, exchanging information

concerns things that you have questions about or that you are worried about

enthusiasm a real excitement and eagerness to do something

feedback information about how someone is doing or behaving

flyers papers that advertise an event or service

responsibility being in charge or held accountable for something

soothe to make someone less anxious or upset, or to ease their worry or pain

sulking grumpy, upset, not wanting to talk

toddlers young children who are learning to walk

yoga a type of exercise that combines stretching, breathing, and simple movements

Index

Be a Better
Babysitter

Annie Buckley
and John Willis

www.av2books.com

AV² provides enriched content that supplements and complements this book. Weigl's AV² books strive to create inspired learning and engage young minds in a total learning experience.

Go to www.av2books.com, and enter this book's unique code.

BOOK CODE

Z947579

AV² by Weigl brings you media enhanced books that support active learning.

Your AV² Media Enhanced books come alive with...

Audio
Listen to sections of the book read aloud.

Video
Watch informative video clips.

Embedded Weblinks
Gain additional information for research.

Try This!
Complete activities and hands-on experiments.

Key Words
Study vocabulary, and complete a matching word activity.

Quizzes
Test your knowledge.

Slide Show
View images and captions, and prepare a presentation.

... and much, much more!

Published by AV² by Weigl
350 5ᵗʰ Avenue, 59ᵗʰ Floor
New York, NY 10118
Website: www.av2books.com

Library of Congress Cataloging-in-Publication Data

Names: Buckley, Annie and Willis, John.
Title: Be a better babysitter / Annie Buckley and John Willis.
Description: New York, NY : AV2 by Weigl, [2017] | Series: Girls rock! |
  Includes index.
Identifiers: LCCN 2016004411 (print) | LCCN 2016008559 (ebook) | ISBN
  9781489647733 (hard cover : alk. paper) | ISBN 9781489650955 (soft cover :
  alk. paper) | ISBN 9781489647740 (Multi-user ebk.)
Subjects: LCSH: Babysitting--Juvenile literature. | Babysitters--Juvenile
  literature.
Classification: LCC HQ769.5 .B83 2017 (print) | LCC HQ769.5 (ebook) | DDC
  649/.10248--dc23
LC record available at http://lccn.loc.gov/2016004411

Printed in the United States of America in Brainerd, Minnesota
1 2 3 4 5 6 7 8 9 0 20 19 18 17 16

042016
041216

Project Coordinator: Katie Gillespie   Designer: Mandy Christiansen

Every reasonable effort has been made to trace ownership and to obtain permission to reprint copyright material. The publishers would be pleased to have any errors or omissions brought to their attention so that they may be corrected in subsequent printings.

Weigl acknowledges Getty Images, iStock, Corbis, and Dreamstime as its primary image suppliers for this title.

Contents

1 Getting Started

You have probably stayed at home with a babysitter when your parents went out. As you get older, you might want to become a babysitter yourself.

This book will give you ideas and information about how you can become a good babysitter. Being a babysitter is a lot of work. It's also a big responsibility. It can be a lot of fun, too!

A babysitter takes care of children while their parents are not at home. Babysitters have the chance to meet new friends, earn extra money, and gain valuable experience.

Remember how much you loved playing with big girls? Now you can be the big girl!

Are you wondering if babysitting is something you want to do? Some things to think about are your age and whether you like to play with younger children.

Most babysitters are about 12 years old or older, but everyone is different. Some kids are ready sooner than others to take on this big responsibility.

If you have younger brothers and sisters, **ask your parents** if you can stay with them for short periods. It's a great way to **learn responsibility.**

People who do the best work enjoy their job, and you will be a better babysitter if you enjoy children and babies.

You have to love hanging out with kids if you want to be a babysitter.

How do you get started? Asking your family and neighbors is a good way. Some kids put up flyers to let others know that they are available to babysit. However you start, remember that the best babysitters act responsibly right from the start.

To be a pro, remember the two C's—caring and communication. A good babysitter cares about the kids she's looking after. She is polite, arrives on time, and follows directions.

She also communicates honestly and clearly with parents and children. She expresses her questions, concerns, and enthusiasm, and she listens to others.

First Steps

Being friendly and talking with the kids you'll sit for is a great first step.

Make sure it's okay with your parents before you ask others about being a babysitter.

Most of the time, a babysitter can handle common problems like a juice spill or an argument over a stuffed bear. She can clean up messes and soothe teary toddlers. But what does a babysitter do in a real emergency?

Just another busy day in the life of a babysitter!

First of all, she keeps her cool and calms the children. Second of all, she knows when to ask for help.

She also plans ahead, keeping a list of important phone numbers in a safe place. These should include the parents' phone, the emergency number 911, and the number of a neighbor.

Safety Tips

- ✔ Keep all doors and windows locked.
- ✔ Don't open the door unless you know the person on the other side.
- ✔ Don't offer information to anyone over the phone or let them know that the parents aren't home.
- ✔ Know where the exits are located.
- ✔ Look for dangerous things, such as sharp objects and cleaning materials, and get them out of the children's reach.

2 The Big Day

A babysitting job feels less like work and more like fun when the babysitter is prepared. Before the parents leave, she writes down emergency numbers, asks the children's names and ages, and listens to any special instructions.

When the parents are out, a prepared babysitter knows where the children are at all times, and she has games and activities ready. Creating a fun and safe environment for children you babysit means more than just showing up!

Make sure to ask the parents questions before they go out.

The first thing to do on any babysitting job is to get to know the children right away. This will go a long way in helping you make babysitting safe and fun.

Play a name game to "break the ice" when you're getting to know the kids.

Here's an idea for a fun way to get to know the children: find a comfortable place and sit in a circle (if the children are wiggly, ask them to hold hands in the circle). One at a time, each child says their name and a funny fact—for instance: a favorite color, an imaginary animal, or a silly word.

Think of interesting questions and let the children think up questions, too. Make sure they are comfortable talking to you and asking you things.

Make the **children** laugh by telling a funny story about **yourself** when you were a kid.

Babies need extra care and more attention than older kids.

You'll probably have to babysit children of different ages as you babysit more. Here are some tips on two ages of kids.

Babies are sweet and cuddly—most of the time—but what if the baby cries? Try picking the baby up, making sure to hold the back of the head for safety. Check if the baby needs a clean diaper or is hungry (use only the food the parents have given you to feed the baby).

Diaper Duty

Be sure to get all the information about diapers before the parents leave the house. If you have never changed a diaper before, ask the parents to show you. Always hold the baby when he or she is on the changing table. Carry the baby when you leave the room. Never leave a baby alone.

Try holding the baby while walking or sitting in a rocking chair. Involve the other kids—they might know what the baby wants.

Toddlers are older, bigger babies. They are just learning to walk, and they teeter and wobble as they go— but they sure enjoy practicing!

Look for games and activities that will keep kids interested and involved.

If you babysit a toddler, be sure to watch him or her all of the time. Keep the room free of sharp objects, and cover the corners of tables with pillows. If you go outside, hold the child's hand so he or she doesn't run off.

Fun and Safety

- ✔ Try to give each child equal attention so no one feels left out.
- ✔ Give kids lots of positive **feedback**— "I love the way you helped your sister!"
- ✔ If you watch TV or listen to music when the children go to sleep, keep the sound low so that you can still hear the children.
- ✔ Keep the children in your sight when they are awake, and once they go to sleep, check on them once in a while.

Babysitting can be fun and full of activity—but remember to balance activity with quiet time. An active game can be followed by something quiet such as reading a book or coloring pictures.

Arrange quiet time for the kids, perhaps by reading to them.

If things are too quiet, liven them up with a fun dance or a game of Simon Says. Before bedtime, quiet time is especially important. It's hard for anyone to go right to sleep after a busy day. You can help smooth the way with a story or soft music.

Quiet and Active Times

Quiet Times
Reading a book, listening to a story, coloring pictures, listening to soft music, talking together about the day, **yoga**, puzzles, relaxing

Active Times
Simon Says, playing tag, dancing to music, musical chairs, red light/green light, group games, singing songs, a tea party

3 More Tips and Ideas

Another part of getting ready for babysitting is putting together your Babysitter's Bag. In a small bag or backpack, put crayons, paper, cards, and a stuffed animal or a ball.

Even if the kids already have these things at their house, the items in your special Babysitter's Bag will be fun and exciting because they are new.

Maybe you have special stickers to give to children who are helpful and cooperative. Most of all, bring your imagination.

A Babysitter's Bag is full of surprises!

What if you prepare your bag, write down the emergency numbers, and are a caring communicator—and things just don't go well? The baby won't stop crying. The 2-year-old twins are fighting. The 8-year-old is sulking. What do you do?

When kids are misbehaving, it is important to stay calm. You can suggest a new activity for them to try instead.

Sometimes, things don't go exactly as we plan. Use all the ideas you can think of to soothe the baby, give equal attention to the twins, and cheer up the 8-year-old. Be ready, however, to accept that things won't always be perfect. Hey, every day can't be sunny! Do your best to be prepared and positive, and don't be afraid to ask for help when you need it.

Unless it is a real emergency, you should usually call the parents first if you need help.

With this book and help from your parents, you can learn to be a great babysitter.

There are lots of ways to be rewarded for your work as a sitter. Some people babysit just because it is fun. Others babysit to help their mom or aunt or a neighbor. In many cases, you can earn money by babysitting.

If you are paid to babysit, make sure to save some money. One good rule is put away half of what you earn.

To find out **how much** you should charge for babysitting, ask around **at school** to see what **other kids** are getting. Usually, you can ask for a certain amount for **every hour** you are there.

Then you can use the other half to get yourself something special. After all . . . you worked hard—you deserve it!

After putting some of your pay in a bank or savings, enjoy a reward for your work!

Do's and Don'ts

DO be responsible—get important phone numbers and ask the parents lots of questions.

DO keep your eye on the kids.

DO stay involved—play games, read books, rock the baby.

DO take care of yourself—bring a good book and a snack.

DO have fun—get to know the kids, find out what they like to do, and enjoy your time with them.

DON'T forget to keep important information in a safe place that you can reach easily.

DON'T sit on the couch watching TV or let the kids out of your sight.

DON'T ever do anything that you are not comfortable with or that feels unsafe—talk to your parents or another adult before you babysit if you have any worries.

Babysitter's Bag

1. Children's book
2. Tissues
3. Deck of cards
4. Crayons
5. Pad of paper
6. Package of modeling clay to do art projects with kids
7. Sweater (for you, in case it's cold)
8. Book or magazine to read (in case the kids go to sleep)
9. Fun stickers to use as rewards for good behavior
10. A picture of yourself when you were a younger kid—children love to see baby pictures!

Quiz

1 When is quiet time the most important?

A: Before bedtime

2 How old are most babysitters?

A: 12 years and older

3 How much of what a babysitter earns should be set aside?

A: Half

4 What should you do when taking a toddler outside?

A: Hold his or her hand

5 What should a babysitter put together before starting their job?

A: A Babysitter's Bag

6 What are the two C's of babysitting?

A: Caring and communication

7 What should babysitters balance quiet time with during the day?

A: Activity

8 What is the first thing that should happen in each babysitting job?

A: Get to know the children

9 What should you do if you listen to music while the children are asleep?

A: Keep the sound low so you can still hear the children

10 What must a good babysitter love to do?

A: Hang out with kids